License & Disclaimer

WELCOME!

You're a busy girl, I'm a busy girl, we're all busy girls!

When it comes to eating healthy, it can be incredibly difficult to find the time to make healthy meals and work out. The reality is, sometimes it's just easier to grab fast food on the way home from work and skip the fitness routine! It's also easy to fall into the crash diet trap that often leads to "fast" weight loss and eating it all back a few weeks later. I've been there many times, friend!

In order to REALLY achieve our goals, the change needs to be consistent and start with our habits. It's important that our healthy eating and fitness regime fit into our lifestyles in a REALISTIC way! For the busy girl, this means easy and quick healthy recipes, having a plan when eating out, and a fitness routine that's efficient and effective.

So welcome, friend, to A Month Of Healthy Eats For The Busy Girl! In just 4 weeks, we'll change the way we eat, think, and work out. Let's dive in and achieve our healthy living goals in a realistic and positive way!

You Can Do This!

Table Of Contents

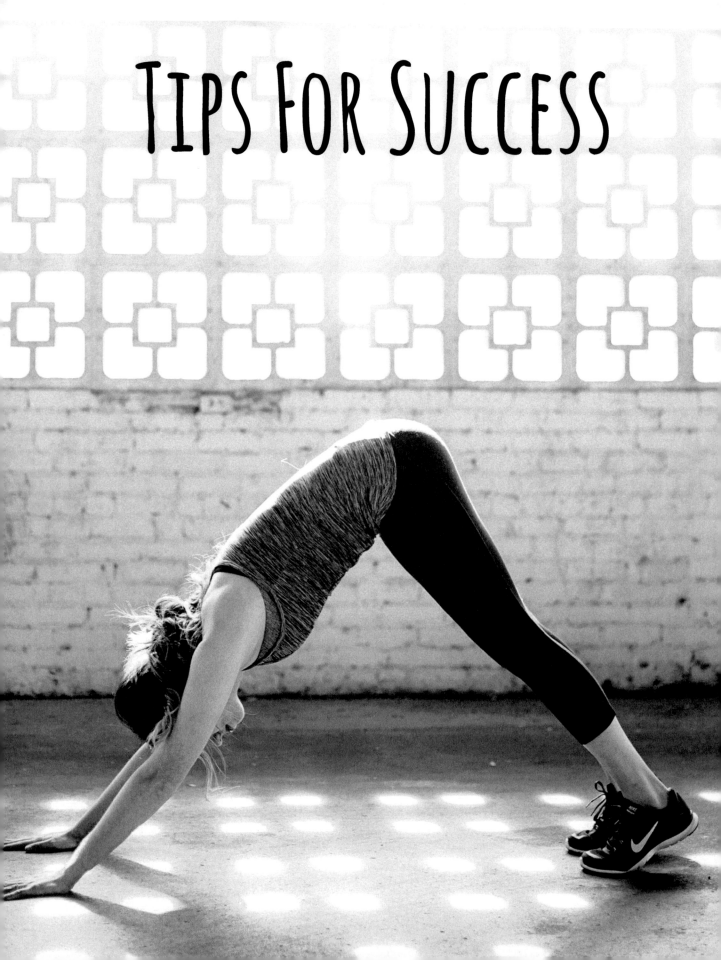

Tips For Success

About The Plan

Healthy living is a combination of healthy eating and fitness. Both are equally important!

The nutrition plan in this 4-week program is designed to be a guide that helps you create (or recreate) healthy eating habits that are both practical and functional.

Each day consists of 3 meals and 3 snacks (one of them is an optional dessert, YAY!). Eating often and throughout the day helps your metabolism and keeps you from getting hungry (which could result in a possible binge later in the day)!

There's also a cheat meal each week (DOUBLE YAY!) because living life is important! Eat anything you want in this meal, but keep in mind that even cheat meals require moderation. In other words, don't make up a week of healthy eating in one meal, but definitely enjoy a splurge. :)

Following The Plan

Follow this plan as closely as possible, but remember that real life happens, too! Never feel guilty about falling off of the plan. Just pick up where you left off! Feel free to switch meals around or write your own meal plan with the availabe recipes as needed.

Calories have also been included in this plan to guide your decisions whenever you need to replace a meal. While calories are definitely NOT the focus of this nutrition plan, each day should fall between 1400 - 1700 calories (except for the splurge meal day).

Next, we'll talk about what to do if you're going out to eat while completing this 4-week nutrition plan!

TIPS FOR EATING OUT

Eating out can be a challenge when you're trying to eat healthy, but with a little planning and a few mindset changes, you can stay on track!

If you're replacing a meal in the nutrition plan with eating out, here are a few tips to stay on track:

1.) Since most of the lunches in this plan are leftovers from dinner, make a plan.

a. <u>When Eating Out For Dinner:</u> Look at your plan and if the next day calls for leftovers, box up HALF of your dinner meal for lunch the next day.

b. <u>When Eating Out For Lunch:</u> If that day's lunch on the plan is leftovers, only make half of the dinner recipe the night before. If it's not leftovers, then simply enjoy a healthy meal out for lunch!

2.) Aim to replace the plan meal with a meal of equivalant calories!

3.) PLAN AHEAD! This is the most important thing for eating out and eating healthy. Look at the menu ahead of time and choose your healthy meal in advance, making sure that you don't stray from your decision when you get there. It's easy to be swayed when temptation is all around you, but you're more likely to stand your ground if you've made up your mind ahead of time!

4.) Think about how the food will *benefit* your body and provide real energy, not about what you're craving. Thinking about all of the healthy foods you *can* have instead of the bad foods you *can't* have is helpful when it comes to making wise food choices on the fly!

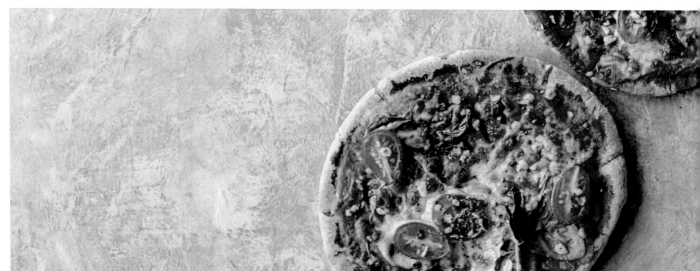

Fitness Plan Overview

In addition to delicious and healthy recipes, we'll be toning up in the 4-week fitness plan! Here's how the fitness plan works:

1. Do the provided workouts 3 times a week.

- Example: Upper body on Monday, core on Wednesday, and lower body on Friday!

- Each workout sheet should be completed at least twice.

- Start with a weight that you can lift, then challenge yourself by adding more weight to the workouts over time!

- Take a 30-45 second break between moves.

- Always listen to your body! Take it slower and reduce weight if needed.

2. Do cardio 3 times a week.

Running, kickboxing, jump rope, or any cardio you want!

3. Take a rest day and stretch!

Rest is SUPER important for recovery, so be sure to take a rest day and stretch out tired muscles!

4. Drink LOTS of water.

Staying hydrated is crucial!

Achieving Your Goals

Stay on track and achieve your goals by doing these simple tasks before starting the plan:

1. Write down your goals

Set goals for the plan, but also set weekly or even daily goals!

2. Take a before (and after) photo!

It's great to know that you've progressed, but it's so fun to see the progress!

3. Write down your measurements

Measure your waist, arms, legs, and hips before you start. Write down your measurements before and after the program!

4. Check your kitchen/buy groceries

Weekly grocery lists are provided, but feel free to add to them! Be sure to add healthy snacks to them and always check your kitchen for items that you may already have.

5. Plan ahead

Look at your plan before the week starts and check your plan every night. Be sure to plan ahead if you're eating out or are substituting meals!

Recipes

BREAKFASTS

Triple Berry Breakfast Parfait (Serves 1)

Ingredients:

1/3 cup plain greek yogurt
1/4 cup granola
1 cup mixed berries

Directions:

Combine the yogurt, granola, and berries. Enjoy!

Apple Crumble Parfait (Serves 1)
from JarOfLemons.com

Ingredients:

1/3 cup plain greek yogurt
1/4 cup granola
1/2 Tbsp honey
1 apple (cubed)

Directions:

Combine the yogurt, granola, honey, and apple. Enjoy!

Peanut Butter Cookie Overnight Oats (Serves 1)

Ingredients:

1/4 cup rolled oats
1 Tbsp peanut butter
1 tsp cinnamon
1/2 tsp stevia
1 tsp maple syrup
2 Tbsp plain greek yogurt
1/2 cup almond milk

Directions:

Mix everything together in a mason jar. Place in refrigerator overnight, then enjoy in the morning!

BREAKFASTS

Blueberry Muffins (Serves 6)

Ingredients:

1/4 cup rolled oats
1/2 tsp baking powder
1/2 Tbsp flaxseed
1/2 Tbsp chia seed
1 egg
2 Tbsp almond butter

1/2 banana
1/2 tsp vanilla
1/4 cup blueberries
4 pitted dates
1/2 tsp cinnamon
pinch of salt

Directions:

Preheat oven to 350 degrees. Blend the rolled oats to create a flour texture. Add in all of the ingredients (except for the blueberries) and blend. Mix in the blueberries by hand. Spray a muffin pan with coconut oil (or use cupcake liners) and pour the batter into the pan. Bake for 30-35 minutes, or until a toothpick comes out clean. Let cool and serve!

Almond Flour Waffles (Serves 4)
from JarOfLemons.com

Ingredients:

2 eggs
2 Tbsp almond milk
1/2 tsp vanilla
1 Tbsp coconut oil
1/2 cup + 2 Tbsp almond flour
1/2 tsp stevia
pinch of salt

Directions:

Oil and preheat your waffle maker. Mix all ingredients together (until the batter is smooth) and pour into waffle maker. Cook until lightly browned. Freeze for later or enjoy immediately!

Pineapple Ginger Smoothie Bowl (Serves 1)

Ingredients:

1 cup frozen
pineapple
1 tsp ground ginger
1 banana
1/4 cup greek yogurt
1/4 cup granola

Directions:

Blend all of the
ingredients together
(except for the
granola). Pour
smoothie into a bowl
and top with granola!

Banana Split Parfait (Serves 1)

Ingredients:

1 banana
1/4 cup plain greek yogurt
1/2 Tbsp honey
1/2 cup berries
1/4 cup granola
1/2 Tbsp chocolate chips

Directions:

Combine everything
in a bowl and enjoy!

Kale Apple Smoothie (Serves 1)

Ingredients:

1 apple
1 cup kale
1 cup ice cubes
1 cup almond milk

Directions:

Blend everything
together and enjoy!

LUNCHES

Rainbow Salad (Serves 1)

Ingredients:

3/4 cup spinach
3 mini sweet peppers
4 grape tomatoes
1/4 cup shredded carrots
1/4 cup chickpeas
1/2 Tbsp olive oil
salt/pepper

Directions:

Chop the spinach, peppers, and tomatoes into small pieces. In a large mason jar, layer the salad upside down (starting w/ the olive oil and ending with the spinach).

Avo Toast (Serves 1)
from JarOfLemons.com

Ingredients:

1 slice sprouted grain bread
1/4 cup spinach
1/2 avocado
4 grape tomatoes
salt/pepper

Directions:

Toast the bread and cut the tomatoes into halves. Top the bread with spinach, avocado slices, tomatoes, and salt/pepper. Enjoy!

Chicken Sandwich (Serves 1)

Ingredients:

3/4 cup leftover chicken
2 slices sprouted grain bread
1/2 cup spinach
4 grape tomatoes
1 tsp mustard
1 cup baby carrots

Directions:

Toast the bread and slice the tomatoes into halves. Fill the sandwich with chicken, spinach, tomatoes, and mustard. Serve the carrots on the side and enjoy!

Greek Chicken Wrap (Serves 1)

Ingredients:

1 flatbread/wrap
1/2 Tbsp olive oil
1 cup spinach
1/2 cup leftover chicken
4 grape tomatoes
1/4 red onion
1/4 cup feta cheese
1/4 cup cucumber slices

Directions:

Slice the cucumber, red onion, and grape tomatoes. Lay a wrap tortilla or flatbread flat and top with olive oil, spinach, leftover chicken, tomatoes, red onion, feta, and cucumber. Enjoy!

Dinners

Slow Cooker Salmon (Serves 1)
from JarOfLemons.com

Ingredients:

1/4 cup dry quinoa
1/4 cup vegetable broth
1 frozen salmon filet
5-6 pieces fresh asparagus
1 cup mushrooms
salt/pepper

Directions:

Thaw the salmon filet ahead of time. Place the filet and quinoa beside each other in a slow cooker. Pour the broth over the quinoa, then top the filet with the asparagus and mushrooms (keeping the veggies from touching the sides of the slow cooker). Add salt/pepper, then cook on low for 2 hours or high for 1 hour. Enjoy!

Roasted Chicken w/ Green Beans & Sweet Potatoes (Serves 1 + Leftover Chicken)

Ingredients:

1 small whole organic chicken
1 cup frozen green beans
1 small sweet potato
Seasoning of choice

Directions:

Preheat oven to 375 degrees. Place the chicken in a small roaster and add 1 inch of water. Spray the chicken with coconut oil and add seasoning of choice. Place lid on roaster and cook for 2.5-3 hours, ensuring the center of the meat is fully cooked (about 180 degrees). Carve the chicken, setting aside a chicken breast. Place the rest of the meat in a container and refrigerate. Steam the sweet potato and green beans, then serve with the set aside chicken breast!

Dinners

Slow Cooker Beef Carnitas Tacos (Serves 2)
from JarOfLemons.com

Ingredients:

6 oz. organic tenderized round steak
2 tsp chili powder
1/4 tsp paprika
1/4 red onion
1/2 tsp garlic
salt/pepper
1/2 Tbsp olive oil
4 corn tortillas

2 Tbsp feta cheese
fresh cilantro
1/2 avocado
1/2 Tbsp yogurt
1 lime

Directions:

Place the olive oil and steak in the slow cooker. Season with chili powder, paprika, 1/8 of the onion (chopped), garlic, and salt/pepper. Cook on high for 1 hour or low for 2 hours. While the meat is cooking, create the dressing by blending the avocado, yogurt, and lime. Once the steak is done, slice into thin slices. Top each tortilla with steak, feta, cilantro, the remaining chopped onion, and dressing. Enjoy 2 tacos with a side salad, then save the other 2 for lunch the next day!

Mexican Quinoa Bowl (Serves 2)

Ingredients:

2 cups spinach
1/4 cup dry quinoa
1/4 cup canned black beans
4 mini peppers (chopped)

1 cup leftover chicken
1/4 cup shredded cheese
1 avocado

Directions:

Cook quinoa according to directions. Heat 1/2 of the chicken. Layer the bowl with 1/2 of everything: spinach, quinoa, beans, peppers, chicken, cheese, and avocado. Save the other 1/2 for lunch the next day (place avo in lemon juice). Enjoy!

Dinners

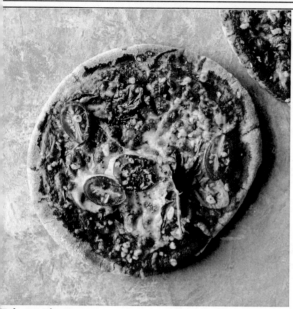

Flatbread Pizza (Serves 1)

Ingredients:

1 flatbread
1/4 cup tomato paste
1 cup spinach
1/4 cup shredded cheese
4-5 grape tomatoes
1 cup leftover chicken (optional)

Directions:

Preheat oven at 350 degrees. Top the flatbread with tomato paste, spinach, shredded cheese, halved grape tomatoes, and optional chicken. Bake 10-15 minutes or until crust is lightly browned and cheese is melted. Enjoy!

Enchilada Casserole (Serves 2)

Ingredients:

1 Tbsp olive oil
4 corn tortillas
2 cups leftover chicken
10 oz. enchilada sauce can
1/2 cup shredded cheese
6 mini peppers
1 cup spinach
cilantro

Directions:

Preheat oven to 350 degrees and spread the olive oil in the bottom of a casserole pan. Tear the tortillas into pieces and spread half of them across the bottom. Pour 1 cup of the sauce over the tortillas, adding 1 cup of the chicken, 1/2 of the chopped peppers, 1/2 of the spinach, and 1/4 cup of shredded cheese. Add another layer of the tortillas and remaining ingredients. Top with cilantro and bake for 15-20 minutes. Enjoy 1/2 of the casserole tonight, then save the rest for lunch tomorrow!

Sriracha Lime Shrimp Tacos (Serves 2)
from JarOfLemons.com

Ingredients:

8 oz. medium shrimp
2 Tbsp green onion
1/4 Tbsp coconut oil
1/2 tsp chili powder
1/2 tsp crushed red pepper
1 tsp soy sauce
1/2 cup shredded red cabbage
1/4 cup shredded carrots
4 corn tortillas
1/2 lime
Salt/pepper
1.5 Tbsp sriracha
1 Tbsp plain greek yogurt
1/2 Tbsp chia seeds

Directions:

In a skillet, lightly stir-fry the green onions in the coconut oil over medium heat. Add in the shrimp and cook. Once the shrimp are done, add in the salt/pepper, red pepper, chili powder and soy sauce. Continue to cook until the soy sauce reduces. While everything is cooking, make the sriracha sauce by blending the sriracha, yogurt, and chia seeds (or mixing them together in a bowl). Top each tortilla with cabbage, carrots, and shrimp. Drizzle with the sauce and lime juice, then top with green onions. Enjoy 2 tacos tonight with a side salad, save the other 2 for lunch tomorrow!

Greek Chicken Flatbread (Serves 1)

Ingredients: salt/pepper

1 flatbread
1/2 Tbsp olive oil
1 cup spinach
1/2 cup leftover chicken
4 grape tomatoes
1/2 cup sliced red onion
4-5 cucumber slices
1/4 cup feta

Directions:

Preheat oven to 350 degrees. Top the flatbread with all of the ingredients. Bake 15-20 minutes and enjoy!

Garlic Chickpea Spaghetti Squash (Serves 2)

Ingredients:

1 small spaghetti squash
10 oz. can chickpeas
1 tsp crushed garlic
8 oz. can tomato sauce
1 cup spinach
1 Tbsp crushed basil
salt/pepper

Directions:

Preheat oven to 375 degrees. Cut the spaghetti squash in half (long ways) and remove the seeds and filling in the middle. Pour a thin layer of water over a baking pan and place each squash half face down. Bake for about 45 minutes. When the squash has about 10 minutes left, mix all of the other ingredients in a sauce pan over medium heat. Keeping the sauce mixture warm, remove the squash from the oven and scrape out the "spaghetti" with a fork. Save half of the spaghetti and sauce mixture for lunch the next day and enjoy half right away!

Slow Cooker Ground Turkey Chili (Serves 2)

Ingredients:

1/2 lb lean ground turkey
1/2 cup dry lentils
2 cups water
1/4 white onion
1 cup chopped mini peppers

1/2 cup tomato sauce
1 Tbsp paprika
1 tsp garlic
2 tsp oregano
1 Tbsp chili powder
salt/pepper

Directions:

Throw all of the ingredients into a slow cooker and cook on low for 3 hours or high for 1 - 1.5 hours (making sure the turkey is fully cooked before eating). Enjoy half of the chili tonight, save the rest for lunch tomorrow!

DINNERS

Margherita Pizza (Serves 1)

Ingredients:

1 flat bread
1/2 Tbsp olive oil
1/4 cup mozzarella
4-5 grape tomatoes
4-5 basil leaves
Italian seasoning
salt/pepper

Directions:

Preheat oven to 350 degrees. Top the flatbread with all of the ingredients, then bake 15-20 minutes. Enjoy!

Ground Turkey Stuffed Sweet Potatoes (Serves 2)

Ingredients:

1/2 lb lean ground turkey
1/2 tsp garlic
Salt/pepper
1 tsp basil

2 sweet potatoes
4 mini peppers
1 cup spinach
1/4 cup shredded cheese

Directions:

Cook the ground turkey in a skillet. Once the turkey is almost fully cooked, add the garlic, seasoning, and chopped mini peppers to the skillet. Continue cooking until the turkey is fully cooked, then leave on low heat to keep warm.

Save one potato for lunch the next day and heat one potato in the microwave for 3 minutes (wash, poke small holes in it, and wrap with a wet towel before microwaving). Slice the potato open, mash the insides, and add half of the spinach, turkey mixture, and shredded cheese. Save the rest for lunch tomorrow!

Nutrition Plan

Week One - Grocery List

Always check to see what you already have in your kitchen!

Fruit

- [ ] 2 Blueberry Containers
- [ ] 2 Raspberry Containers
- [ ] 2 Blackberry Containers
- [ ] 6 Bananas
- [ ] 2 Apples
- [ ] 1 Container Dates

Veggies

- [ ] 1 Large Bag Spinach
- [ ] 1 Bag Mini Peppers
- [ ] 1 Small Bag Shredded Carrots
- [ ] 1 Container Grape Tomatoes
- [ ] 1 Cup Fresh Asparagus
- [ ] 1 Container Mushrooms
- [ ] 2 Avocados (3 if making optional Avocado Lime Dressing)
- [ ] 2 Medium Sweet Potatoes
- [ ] 1 Red Onion
- [ ] 1 Bunch Cilantro
- [ ] 1 Red Cabbage
- [ ] 1 Small Bag Baby Carrots
- [ ] 2 Limes (3 if making optional Avocado Lime Dressing)
- [ ] 1 Small Container Crushed Garlic
- [ ] Green Onions

Meat

- [x] 1 Wild-Caught Salmon Filet
- [ ] 2 Small Organic Fryer Chickens
- [ ] 6 Oz. Organic, Grass-Fed Tenderized Round Steak
- [x] 8 Oz. Medium Shrimp

Dairy

- [ ] 1 Bag Organic Shredded Cheese
- [ ] Feta Cheese
- [ ] 35 oz. Container Nonfat Plain Greek Yogurt
- [ ] 1/2 Dozen Eggs
- [ ] Milk Of Choice

Frozen

- [ ] Sprouted Grain Bread
- [ ] Frozen Green Beans

Other

- [ ] 8 Corn Tortillas
- [x] Honey
- [x] Maple Syrup
- [ ] Almond Butter
- [x] Peanut Butter
- [x] Mustard
- [ ] 1 Bag Granola
- [ ] Rolled Oats
- [ ] Bran Cereal
- [x] 1 Bag Quinoa
- [x] Ground Flaxseed
- [x] Chia Seeds
- [ ] Stevia
- [x] Baking Powder
- [x] Vanilla
- [ ] 8 oz. Can Black Beans
- [ ] 8 oz. Can Chickpeas
- [ ] 8 Oz. Can Broth
- [x] Soy Sauce
- [x] Sriracha
- [ ] Lite Popcorn
- [ ] Mixed Nuts
- [ ] 3 Protein Bars

Oils/Spices

- [x] Cinnamon
- [x] Coconut Oil
- [x] Crushed Red Pepper
- [x] Chili Powder
- [x] Paprika
- [x] Olive Oil
- [x] Salt/Pepper

Monday

- ☐ Triple Berry Breakfast Parfait - 258
- ☐ Banana - 120
- ☐ Rainbow Salad - 179
- ☐ Protein Bar - 230
- ☐ Slow Cooker Salmon - 398
- ☐ Snack Of Choice - 300

Total Calories: 1485

Tuesday

- ☐ Bran Cereal, Berries, Milk - 281
- ☐ Handful Mixed Nuts - 170
- ☐ Avo Toast - 203
- ☐ Popcorn - 100
- ☐ Roasted Chicken w/ Green Beans, Sweet Potato, & Avo - 497
- ☐ Snack Of Choice - 200

Total Calories: 1451

NOTES: SAVE 1/2 OF THE AVO FROM THE AVO TOAST IN A BAG W/ LEMON JUICE FOR DINNER LATER TONIGHT! FOR DINNER TONIGHT, EAT ONE SERVING OF CHICKEN AND 1/2 OF THE GREEN BEANS/ SWEET POTATO. SET ASIDE THE OTHER CHICKEN BREAST AND LEFTOVER VEGETABLES FOR LUNCH TOMORROW, THEN REFRIGERATE THE LEFTOVER MEAT FOR RECIPES THROUGHOUT THE WEEK.

Wednesday

- ☐ Apple Crumble Parfait - 310
- ☐ Banana - 120
- ☐ Leftovers from Tuesday's Dinner - 336
- ☐ Protein Bar - 230
- ☐ Slow Cooker Beef Carnitas Tacos - 367
- ☐ Snack Of Choice - 200

Total Calories: 1563

Thursday

- ☐ Bran Cereal, Berries, Milk - 281
- ☐ Handful Mixed Nuts - 170
- ☐ Leftovers from Wednesday's Dinner - 367
- ☐ Banana + 1 T Almond Butter - 200
- ☐ Mexican Quinoa Bowl - 336
- ☐ Snack Of Choice - 200

Total Calories: 1554

Friday

- ☐ Peanut Butter Overnight Oats - 194
- ☐ Apple - 80
- ☐ Leftover from Thursday's Dinner - 336
- ☐ Protein Bar - 230
- ☐ Splurge Meal! (or Flatbread Pizza)
- ☐ Snack Of Choice - 200

Total Calories: 1500 - 2300

Saturday

- ☐ 3 Blueberry Muffins - 270
- ☐ Banana + 1 T Almond Butter - 200
- ☐ Chicken Sandwich - 253
- ☐ Popcorn - 100
- ☐ Sriracha Lime Shrimp Tacos - 360
- ☐ Snack Of Choice - 300

Total Calories: 1483

Sunday

- ☐ Bran Cereal, Berries, Milk - 281
- ☐ Handful Mixed Nuts - 170
- ☐ Leftovers Saturday's Dinner - 360
- ☐ Banana + 1 T Almond Butter - 200
- ☐ Roasted Chicken w/ Green Beans & Sweet Potato - 336
- ☐ Snack Of Choice - 200

Total Calories: 1547

NOTES: SEE TUESDAY'S NOTE!

20

Week Two - Grocery List

Always check to see what you already have in your kitchen!

Fruit

- [ ] 5 Apples
- [ ] 5 Bananas
- [ ] 1 Strawberry or 2 Raspberry Containers
- [ ] 2 Blueberry Containers
- [ ] 2 Blackberry Containers

Veggies

- [ ] 2 Bags Spinach
- [ ] 1 Bag Mini Sweet Peppers
- [ ] 1 Bag Shredded Carrots
- [ ] 1 Container Grape Tomatoes
- [ ] 1 Red Onion
- [ ] 3 Mini Cucumbers
- [ ] 2 Avocados (3 if making optional Avocado Lime Dressing)
- [ ] 1 Small White Onion
- [ ] 1 Bunch Cilantro
- [ ] 1 Small Kale Bunch
- [ ] 1 Lime (optional for Avocado Lime Dressing)
- [ ] 1 Spaghetti Squash

Meat

- [ ] 6 Oz. Organic, Grass-Fed Tenderized Round Steak
- [ ] 1/2 lb Lean Ground Turkey

Dairy

- [ ] 1 Bag Organic Shredded Cheese
- [ ] Feta Cheese
- [ ] Medium Container Nonfat Plain Greek Yogurt
- [ ] Milk Of Choice

Frozen

- [ ] Frozen Pineapple

Other

- [ ] 8 Corn Tortillas
- [ ] 3 Flatbreads
- [ ] Almond Butter
- [ ] Honey
- [ ] Bran Cereal
- [ ] 1 Bag Granola
- [ ] Mini Dark Chocolate Chips
- [ ] 1 Bag Quinoa
- [ ] Dry Lentils
- [ ] 2 8 oz. Cans Tomato Sauce
- [ ] 16 oz. Can Enchilada Sauce
- [ ] 1 Can Black Beans
- [ ] 1 8 oz. Can Chickpeas
- [ ] 1 10 oz. Can Chickpeas
- [ ] Lite Popcorn
- [ ] Mixed Nuts
- [ ] 3 Protein Bars

Oils/Spices

- [ ] Chili Powder
- [ ] Ground Ginger
- [ ] Paprika
- [ ] Oregano
- [ ] Italian Seasoning or Basil
- [ ] Crushed Garlic
- [ ] Olive Oil

Add Your Own Snacks!

- [ ] _____
- [ ] _____
- [ ] _____
- [ ] _____
- [ ] _____
- [ ] _____
- [ ] _____
- [ ] _____

Week Two - Plan

Monday
- [ ] Leftover Blueberry Muffins - 270
- [ ] Apple - 80
- [ ] Rainbow Salad + 1 C Chicken - 279
- [ ] Popcorn - 100
- [ ] Enchilada Casserole - 516
- [ ] Snack Of Choice - 200

Total Calories: 1445

Tuesday
- [ ] Pineapple Ginger Smoothie - 361
- [ ] Banana - 120
- [ ] Leftovers from Monday's Dinner - 516
- [ ] Apple - 80
- [ ] Greek Chicken Flatbread - 386
- [ ] Snack Of Choice - 200

Total Calories: 1663

Wednesday
- [ ] Bran Cereal, Berries, Milk - 281
- [ ] Apple - 80
- [ ] Greek Chicken Wraps - 322
- [ ] Banana + 1 T Almond Butter -200
- [ ] Slow Cooker Beef Carnitas Tacos - 367
- [ ] Snack Of Choice - 300

Total Calories: 1550

Thursday
- [ ] Triple Berry Breakfast Parfait - 258
- [ ] Mixed Nuts - 170
- [ ] Leftovers from Wednesday's Dinner - 367
- [ ] Protein Bar - 230
- [ ] Slow Cooker Turkey Chili - 312
- [ ] Snack Of Choice - 200

Total Calories: 1537

Friday
- [ ] Banana Split Parfait - 298
- [ ] 1 C Berries - 100
- [ ] Leftover from Thursday's Dinner - 312
- [ ] Popcorn - 100
- [ ] Splurge Meal! (or Flatbread Pizza)
- [ ] Snack Of Choice - 200

Total Calories: 1500 - 2300

Saturday
- [ ] Bran Cereal, Berries, Milk - 281
- [ ] Apple - 80
- [ ] Mexican Quinoa Bowl - 336
- [ ] Protein Bar - 230
- [ ] Greek Chicken Flatbread - 386
- [ ] Snack Of Choice - 200

Total Calories: 1513

Sunday
- [ ] Kale Apple Smoothie - 190
- [ ] Banana + 1 T Almond Butter - 200
- [ ] Leftover Mexican Quinoa Bowl - 336
- [ ] Protein Bar - 230
- [ ] Garlic Chickpea & Spaghetti Squash - 243
- [ ] Snack Of Choice - 300

Total Calories: 1499

Week Three - Grocery List

Always check to see what you already have in your kitchen!

Fruit

- [ ] 1 Blueberry Container
- [ ] 1 Raspberry or Strawberry Container
- [ ] 1 Blackberry Containers
- [ ] 4 Bananas
- [ ] 4 Apples
- [ ] Frozen Pineapple

Veggies

- [ ] 2 Bags Spinach
- [ ] 1 Bag Mini Peppers
- [ ] 1 Small Bag Shredded Carrots
- [ ] 1 Container Grape Tomatoes
- [ ] 1 Cup Asparagus
- [ ] 1 Container Mushrooms
- [ ] 1 Mini Cucumber
- [ ] 3 Small Sweet Potatoes
- [ ] 1 Red Onion
- [ ] 1 Bunch Cilantro
- [ ] 1 Red Cabbage
- [ ] 1 Small Bag Baby Carrots
- [ ] 1 Lime
- [ ] 1 Small Container Crushed Garlic
- [ ] Fresh Basil Leaves

Meat

- [ ] 1 Wild-Caught Salmon Filet
- [ ] 1 Small Organic Fryer Chicken
- [ ] 8 Oz. Medium Shrimp
- [ ] 1/2 lb Lean Ground Turkey

Dairy

- [ ] 1 Bag Organic Shredded Cheese
- [ ] Feta Cheese
- [ ] 1/2 Dozen Eggs
- [ ] 1 Small Bag Shredded Mozzarella
- [ ] Medium Container Nonfat Plain Greek Yogurt
- [ ] Milk Of Choice

Frozen

- [ ] Sprouted Grain Bread
- [ ] Frozen Green Beans
- [ ] 2 Flatbreads
- [ ] 2 Frozen Meals

Other

- [ ] 6 Corn Tortillas
- [ ] Bran Cereal
- [ ] 1 Bag Granola
- [ ] Rolled Oats
- [ ] Maple Syrup
- [ ] Honey
- [ ] Almond Butter
- [ ] Peanut Butter
- [ ] 1 Bag Quinoa
- [ ] Chia Seeds
- [ ] Stevia
- [ ] 1 Small Bag Almond Flour
- [ ] Soy Sauce
- [ ] Sriracha
- [ ] 1 4 oz. Can Broth
- [ ] 16 oz. Can Enchilada Sauce
- [ ] 1 Bag Pita Chips
- [ ] Hummus
- [ ] Lite Popcorn
- [ ] Mixed Nuts
- [ ] 2 Protein Bars

Oils/Spices

- [ ] Coconut Oil
- [ ] Olive Oil
- [ ] Ground Ginger
- [ ] Crushed Red Pepper
- [ ] Chili Powder

Add Your Own Snacks!

- [ ] _____
- [ ] _____
- [ ] _____

WEEK THREE - PLAN

Monday
- [ ] Peanut Butter Cookie Overnight Oats - 194
- [ ] Apple - 80
- [ ] Leftovers From Sunday's Dinner - 243
- [ ] Hummus + Pita Chips - 200
- [ ] Slow Cooker Salmon - 398
- [ ] Snack Of Choice - 300

Total Calories: 1415

Tuesday
- [ ] Apple Crumble Parfait - 310
- [ ] 1 Cup Berries - 100
- [ ] Frozen Meal - 300
- [ ] Protein Bar - 230
- [ ] Roasted Chicken w/ Green Beans, Sweet Potato - 336
- [ ] Snack Of Choice - 200

Total Calories: 1476

Wednesday
- [ ] Bran Cereal, Berries, Milk - 281
- [ ] Apple - 80
- [ ] Greek Chicken Wrap - 322
- [ ] Banana + Almond Butter - 200
- [ ] Enchilada Casserole - 516
- [ ] Snack Of Choice - 200

Total Calories: 1599

Thursday
- [ ] Triple Berry Breakfast Parfait - 258
- [ ] Banana - 120
- [ ] Leftovers from Wednesday's Dinner - 516
- [ ] Popcorn - 100
- [ ] Margherita Pizza - 315
- [ ] Snack Of Choice -200

Total Calories: 1509

Friday
- [ ] Pineapple Ginger Smoothie - 361
- [ ] Mixed Nuts - 170
- [ ] Frozen Meal - 300
- [ ] Hummus + Pita Chips - 200
- [ ] Splurge Meal! (or Flatbread Pizza)
- [ ] Snack Of Choice - 200

Total Calories: 1500 - 2300

Saturday
- [ ] Almond Flour Waffles - 212
- [ ] Apple - 80
- [ ] Chicken Sandwich - 324
- [ ] Popcorn - 100
- [ ] Sriracha Lime Shrimp Tacos - 360
- [ ] Snack Of Choice - 400

Total Calories: 1476

Sunday
- [ ] Leftover Almond Flour Waffles - 212
- [ ] Banana - 120
- [ ] Leftovers from Saturday's Dinner - 360
- [ ] Protein Bar - 230
- [ ] Ground Turkey Stuffed Sweet Potatoes - 326
- [ ] Snack Of Choice - 300

Total Calories: 1548

Week Four - Grocery List

Always check to see what you already have in your kitchen!

Fruit

- [ ] 2 Blueberry Containers
- [ ] 1 Raspberry or Strawberry Container
- [ ] 1 Blackberry Container
- [ ] 6 Bananas
- [ ] 3 Apples
- [ ] 1 Container Dates

Veggies

- [ ] 2 Bags Spinach
- [ ] 1 Bag Mini Peppers
- [ ] 1 Small Bag Shredded Carrots
- [ ] 1 Container Grape Tomatoes
- [ ] 1 Small Bag Kale
- [ ] 1 Mini Cucumber
- [ ] 3 Avocados (4 if making optional Avocado Lime Dressing)
- [ ] 1 Sweet Potatoes
- [ ] 1 Red Onion
- [ ] 1 Bunch Cilantro
- [ ] 1 Small Bag Baby Carrots
- [ ] 1 Small White Onion
- [ ] 1 Lime (optional for Avocado Lime Dressing)
- [ ] 1 Small Container Crushed Garlic

Meat

- [ ] 1/2 lb Lean Ground Turkey
- [ ] 1 Small Organic Fryer Chicken
- [ ] 6 Oz. Organic, Grass-Fed Tenderized Round Steak

Dairy

- [ ] 1 Small Bag Shredded Mozzarella
- [ ] 1 Bag Organic Shredded Cheese
- [ ] Feta Cheese
- [ ] 35 oz. Container Nonfat Plain Greek Yogurt
- [ ] 1/2 Dozen Eggs
- [ ] Milk Of Choice

Frozen

- [ ] Sprouted Grain Bread
- [ ] Frozen Green Beans
- [ ] Frozen Pineapple

Other

- [ ] 4 Corn Tortillas
- [ ] 2 Flatbreads
- [ ] Maple Syrup
- [ ] 1 Bag Granola
- [ ] Bran Cereal
- [ ] Rolled Oats
- [ ] Almond Butter
- [ ] Peanut Butter
- [ ] Stevia
- [ ] Chia Seeds
- [ ] Ground Flaxseed
- [ ] 1 Bag Quinoa
- [ ] 1 Small Bag Dry Lentils
- [ ] 8oz. Can Black Beans
- [ ] 8oz. Can Chickpeas
- [ ] 8 oz. Can Tomato Sauce
- [ ] 1 Bag Pita Chips
- [ ] Small Container Hummus
- [ ] Lite Popcorn
- [ ] Mixed Nuts
- [ ] 2 Protein Bars

Oils/Spices

- [ ] Italian Seasoning
- [ ] Chili Powder
- [ ] Paprika
- [ ] Oregano
- [ ] Ground Ginger
- [ ] Olive Oil

Add Your Own Snacks!

- [ ] _____
- [ ] _____
- [ ] _____
- [ ] _____

Week Four - Plan

Monday
- [ ] Kale Apple Smoothie - 190
- [ ] Mixed Nuts - 170
- [ ] Leftovers from Sunday's Dinner - 326
- [ ] Protein Bar - 230
- [ ] Roasted Chicken w/ Green Beans & Sweet Potato - 336
- [ ] Snack Of Choice - 200

Total Calories: 1452

Tuesday
- [ ] Triple Berry Breakfast Parfait - 258
- [ ] Banana - 120
- [ ] Rainbow Salad + 1 C Chicken - 279
- [ ] Hummus + Pita Chips - 200
- [ ] Slow Cooker Beef Carnitas Tacos - 367
- [ ] Snack Of Choice - 300

Total Calories: 1524

Wednesday
- [ ] Bran Cereal, Berries, Milk - 281
- [ ] Apple - 80
- [ ] Greek Chicken Wrap - 322
- [ ] Banana + Almond Butter - 200
- [ ] Leftovers from Tuesday's Dinner - 367
- [ ] Snack Of Choice - 300

Total Calories: 1550

Thursday
- [ ] Peanut Butter Cookie Overnight Oats - 194
- [ ] Banana - 120
- [ ] Chicken Sandwich - 324
- [ ] Hummus + Pita Chips - 200
- [ ] Slow Cooker Ground Chili - 312
- [ ] Snack Of Choice - 300

Total Calories: 1450

Friday
- [ ] Bran Cereal, Berries, Milk - 281
- [ ] Mixed Nuts - 170
- [ ] Leftovers from Thursday's Dinner - 312
- [ ] Banana + Almond Butter - 200
- [ ] Splurge Meal! (or Flatbread Pizza)
- [ ] Snack Of Choice - 200

Total Calories: 1500 - 2300

Saturday
- [ ] 3 Blueberry Muffins - 270
- [ ] Apple - 80
- [ ] Chicken Sandwich - 324
- [ ] Protein Bar - 230
- [ ] Margherita Pizza - 315
- [ ] Snack Of Choice - 200

Total Calories: 1419

Sunday
- [ ] Pineapple Ginger Smoothie - 361
- [ ] Mixed Nuts - 170
- [ ] Avo Toast - 203
- [ ] Popcorn - 100
- [ ] Mexican Quinoa Bowl - 336
- [ ] Snack Of Choice - 300

Total Calories: 1470

Fitness Plan

— WEEK 1 —
UPPER BODY WORKOUT
(DO THIS WORKOUT 2-3 TIMES!)

JAB CROSS KNEE

30 REPS (ALTERNATING)

HIGH KNEES

50 REPS (ALTERNATING)

PUSH UPS

15 REPS

MOUNTAIN CLIMBERS

40 REPS (ALTERNATING)

TRICEP DIPS

15 REPS

TOE TOUCHES

12 REPS (ALTERNATING)

BURPEES

10 REPS

TRICEP EXTENSIONS

20 REPS

WEEK 1
CORE WORKOUT
(DO THIS WORKOUT 2-3 TIMES!)

MOUNTAIN CLIMBERS

30 REPS (ALTERNATING)

HIGH KNEES

50 REPS (ALTERNATING)

CRUNCHES

25 REPS

TOE REACH

15 REPS

PLANK

1 MIN

FROG JUMPS

15 REPS

SIDE PLANKS W/ TWIST

12 REPS EACH SIDE

BUTTERFLY JACK-KNIFE

15 REPS

WEEK 1
LOWER BODY WORKOUT
(DO THIS WORKOUT 2-3 TIMES!)

SIDE LUNGE JUMPS

20 REPS
(ALTERNATING)

SQUAT KICK

20 REPS
(ALTERNATING)
5-10 LBS

SQUAT TO ATTITUDE
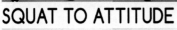

20 REPS
(ALTERNATING)
5-10 LBS

BRIDGE

20 REPS

SQUAT JUMPS

15 REPS

FROG JUMPS

15 REPS

LUNGES

15 REPS
(ALTERNATING)
5-10 LBS

BUTTERFLY

15 REPS
EACH SIDE

JAB CROSS KNEE

40 REPS (ALTERNATING)

HIGH KNEES

50 REPS (ALTERNATING)

PUSH UPS

20 REPS

MOUNTAIN CLIMBERS

50 REPS (ALTERNATING)

TRICEP DIPS

20 REPS

TOE TOUCHES

16 REPS (ALTERNATING)

BURPEES

15 REPS

TRICEP EXTENSIONS

20 REPS

WEEK 2
CORE WORKOUT
(DO THIS WORKOUT 2-3 TIMES!)

MOUNTAIN CLIMBERS

40 REPS (ALTERNATING)

HIGH KNEES

50 REPS (ALTERNATING)

CRUNCHES

30 REPS

TOE REACH

20 REPS

PLANK

1 MIN

FROG JUMPS

20 REPS

SIDE PLANKS W/ TWIST

15 REPS EACH SIDE

BUTTERFLY JACK-KNIFE

20 REPS

WEEK 2
LOWER BODY WORKOUT
(DO THIS WORKOUT 2-3 TIMES!)

SIDE LUNGE JUMPS

30 REPS (ALTERNATING)

SQUAT KICK

24 REPS (ALTERNATING) 5-10 LBS

SQUAT TO ATTITUDE

24 REPS (ALTERNATING) 5-10 LBS

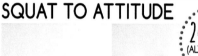

BRIDGE

25 REPS

SQUAT JUMPS

20 REPS

FROG JUMPS

20 REPS

LUNGES

20 REPS (ALTERNATING) 5-10 LBS

BUTTERFLY

20 REPS EACH SIDE

WEEK 3
UPPER BODY WORKOUT
(DO THIS WORKOUT 2-3 TIMES!)

WEIGHTED BURPEES

15 REPS
5-10 LBS

TOE TOUCHES

20 REPS
(ALTERNATING)

DOWNWARD DOG PLANKS

20 REPS
(ALTERNATING)

MOUNTAIN CLIMBERS

50 REPS
(ALTERNATING)

BICEP CURLS

20 REPS
5-10 LBS

SHOULDER PRESS

15 REPS
5-10 LBS

PUSH UPS

20 REPS

TRICEP EXTENSIONS

20 REPS
5-10 LBS

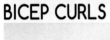

WEEK 3
CORE WORKOUT
(DO THIS WORKOUT 2-3 TIMES!)

HIGH KNEES

50 REPS (ALTERNATING)

MOUNTAIN CLIMBERS

40 REPS (ALTERNATING)

BICYCLE CRUNCHES

24 REPS (ALTERNATING)

TOE REACHES

20 REPS

SIDE PLANKS W/ TWIST

20 REPS EACH SIDE

CRUNCHES

40 REPS

FROG JUMPS

20 REPS

BUTTERFLY JACK-KNIFE

25 REPS

— WEEK 3 —
LOWER BODY WORKOUT
(DO THIS WORKOUT 2-3 TIMES!)

SIDE LUNGE JUMPS

30 REPS (ALTERNATING)

WALKING LUNGES

20 REPS (ALTERNATING) 10-15 LBS

RAISED LEG BRIDGE

15 REPS EACH SIDE

SQUAT JUMPS

20 REPS

LUNGE KICKS

24 REPS (ALTERNATING) 10-15 LBS

BUTTERFLY

20 REPS EACH SIDE

DEEP SQUATS

20 REPS

SQUAT TO ATTITUDE

15 REPS EACH SIDE

— WEEK 4 —
UPPER BODY WORKOUT
(DO THIS WORKOUT 2-3 TIMES!)

WEIGHTED BURPEES

20 REPS
5-10 LBS

DOWNWARD DOG PLANKS

24 REPS
(ALTERNATING)

BICEP CURLS

20 REPS
8-15 LBS

PUSH UPS

20 REPS

TOE TOUCHES

24 REPS
(ALTERNATING)

MOUNTAIN CLIMBERS

50 REPS
(ALTERNATING)

SHOULDER PRESS

15 REPS
8-15 LBS

TRICEP EXTENSIONS

20 REPS
8-15 LBS

WEEK 4
CORE WORKOUT
(DO THIS WORKOUT 2-3 TIMES!)

HIGH KNEES

50 REPS (ALTERNATING)

MOUNTAIN CLIMBERS

50 REPS (ALTERNATING)

BICYCLE CRUNCHES

30 REPS (ALTERNATING)

TOE REACHES

25 REPS

SIDE PLANKS W/ TWIST

24 REPS EACH SIDE

CRUNCHES

50 REPS

FROG JUMPS

25 REPS

BUTTERFLY JACK-KNIFE

30 REPS

— WEEK 4 —
LOWER BODY WORKOUT
(DO THIS WORKOUT 2-3 TIMES!)

SIDE LUNGE JUMPS

40 REPS (ALTERNATING)

WALKING LUNGES

24 REPS (ALTERNATING) 10-15 LBS

RAISED LEG BRIDGE

20 REPS EACH SIDE

SQUAT JUMPS

30 REPS

LUNGE KICKS

30 REPS (ALTERNATING) 10-15 LBS

BUTTERFLY

24 REPS EACH SIDE

DEEP SQUATS

25 REPS

SQUAT TO ATTITUDE

20 REPS EACH SIDE

Where To Go From Here

Congrats! You've completed A Month Of Healthy Eats For The Busy Girl!

So what now?

Incorporate some of these recipes and workouts into your daily routine, but be flexible!

Try to eat healthy based on what you've learned and the foods that you know add energy and nutrition to your body. Do the type of workouts you love, and look for balance in your routine. There are also tons of recipes and workouts on JarOfLemons.com to keep you motivated!

At the end of the day, it's about finding out what works for YOU and sticking with it. Look for balance in living REAL life, but do your best to eat healthy, stay fit, and enjoy life.

Great job and congrats on completing the program! Here's to a healthy future and well balanced life!

About Christine

I'm Christine McMichael, the author behind A Month Of Healthy Eats For The Busy Girl and the blogger behind Jar Of Lemons!

I'm from west Texas and have an amazing husband named Cody. We love to make creative and healthy meals, stay active, and spend time outside whenever the weather is nice!

I also love inspiring women to be the healthiest version of themselves through a realistic and practical approach. I'm all about easy recipes, efficient workouts, and living life to the fullest!

If you have enjoyed A Month Of Healthy Eats For The Busy Girl, be sure to check out Jar Of Lemons (JarOfLemons.com) for healthy, easy recipes and efficient workouts! I always love seeing what you guys are cooking up and love connecting with each and every one of you!

Made in the USA
San Bernardino, CA
07 April 2019